Alfons Unmüßig

The Human Being as Key Element for Software Process Improvement

GRIN Verlag

Bibliografische Information der Deutschen Nationalbibliothek:

Die Deutsche Bibliothek verzeichnet diese Publikation in der Deutschen National-
bibliografie; detaillierte bibliografische Daten sind im Internet über http://dnb.d-
nb.de/ abrufbar.

Imprint:

Copyright © 2012 GRIN Verlag GmbH
Druck und Bindung: Books on Demand GmbH, Norderstedt Germany
ISBN: 978-3-656-34475-9

This book at GRIN:

http://www.grin.com/en/e-book/203115/the-human-being-as-key-element-for-
software-process-improvement

GRIN - Your knowledge has value

Der GRIN Verlag publiziert seit 1998 wissenschaftliche Arbeiten von Studenten, Hochschullehrern und anderen Akademikern als eBook und gedrucktes Buch. Die Verlagswebsite www.grin.com ist die ideale Plattform zur Veröffentlichung von Hausarbeiten, Abschlussarbeiten, wissenschaftlichen Aufsätzen, Dissertationen und Fachbüchern.

The Human being as key element of Software Process Improvement

- The Human being is the most interlinked influence element in Software Process Improvement   -

Contens

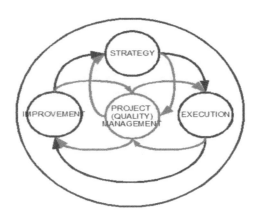

Abstract

This paper aims to explain a new approach of software process improvements (SPI). The approach will not replace the existing methods, but will support them for SPI from an additional view. The additional view consists the SPI as a networked system of the activities for SPI. The approach is an extract of a comprehensive PhD paper about SPI and defect prevention from the author. In the PhD paper the author is using over 100 important influence elements. The title of the PhD paper is: „Ganzheitlich vernetzte Fehlerprävention im Software-Entwicklungsprozess." (Unmüßig 2012)

Today there are various actions and constructive methods in software process improvements used. As there are a lot of different elements and subjects in the process of improvements involved - it is a complex process. The most involved elements and subjects are e.g. the human being (management, members of staff, customer, work psychology), methods, organisations, culture etc. The author's own experience and studies confirm that the human being is one of the most important elements in the process. The human being is much more involved in the process than considered in the daily work today. His work performance e.g. software process improvements depends on a lot of interlinked factors.

This paper will use an excerpt of 12 important elements of the above mentioned PhD paper. The elements will be interlinked. A software tool is used to interlink, present and simulate the interrelationship to the other elements. The approach and results can be used in all software process improvements (SPI) / software development processes to support the existing SPI approaches and measures. The support is based on the position (strengths) and relationship of the elements in the result matrix.

Keywords: Software, Software development, Software development process, Software process improvement, SPI, Software quality, holistic, human being, human factors, interlinked elements, Influence factors, defect prevention, processes, methods, organisation, culture, network thinking, SPI Manifesto.

1 Introduction

Today's software process improvement techniques have made substantial progress over the last years in a contribution to better software quality, but this is not enough.

The new approach consist 12 important elements/activities of SPI elements in a complex System. Today the elements e.g. methods, procedure are mostly technical elements (hard facts). Soft facts are not in the focus and both facts are not interlinked.

The key focus in the new approach in the Software Development Process is on Requirement Analysis and Specification. Based on the results of the research of available sources and in the author's own experience, 50 to 70 % of all failures come about in these two first development phases (Masing 2007). At present, software is still prevalently compiled by humans. This means the key failure source for SW errors are human factors. The paper will present some interlinked aspects for Software Process Improvement (SPI).

2   Software Development

Process / Procedure Models

For the development of software, methods, process and procedure models are in use (see Fig. 1). The activities and results fall under different types of operations such as project management. Process models further also define the relevant roles, tools and methods (Wallmüller 2001). Figure 1 shows the SW Development process and one of the various process / procedure models.

● Phases of Software Development Process

Requirements- analysis	Design	Implemen- tation	Modul- test	Integration- test	System- test	Field use	Improve- ments

● Procedure Models for SW Development

   - Waterfallmodel, V- Model, V-Model 97

   - Spiralmodel

   - and others

● Procedure Models describe

   - Procedure

   - Methods

   - Tools-Requirements

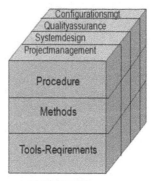

V- Model 97

● Comprehensive Systemic Failure Prevention requests
an new approach/ model

FIG. 1: Software Development Process; (source: Relating to Hindel 2009)

Process / procedure models outline the applicable organisational framework and the sequence within the software development process. As synonyms to procedure model according to (Masing 2007, p. 824), terms such as software lifecycle, phase model, project model or process model also apply, organisational framework includes the following aspects (Balzert 1998, p. 38):

- The partial actions and sequence thereof within the process sequence (project phases);
- Planned schedules;
- Required employee qualification;
- Applicable standards, references, directives, tools and techniques.

Different procedure models emerged out of the framework conditions. The differences between the procedure models mainly relate to the level of complexity, the number of phases and the sequence of steps within procedures. The complexity of an adequate procedure model depends on circumstances in each particular case.

3 Software Process Improvement (SPI) Methods

There are various Software Process Improvement-Methods (SPI-M) used today.

3.1 Actions

1. Analytical Quality Actions
Analytical quality actions are implemented e.g. in order to verify current quality levels. The examinations do not establish absolute certainty regarding conformity/non-conformity of a product.
There are e.g. following analytical quality actions used: white box test, black box test and cause-effect analysis.

2. Constructive Quality Actions
Constructive quality actions mainly aim at defect prevention. For e.g. procedure/process models, methods, program language, quality gates, Risk management, Personal & Team Software process (PSP / TSP), FMEA & Reviews.

3. Organizational Quality Actions
Organizational actions include the design, implementation and maintenance of e.g. a corporate Quality Management System, Project Management System, team-building and others.

4. Psychological Prevention Actions/People Actions
Software development should not be considered a purely technical procedure only. As software development is carried by the human input (the development team), communication processes, leadership, quality culture and other variables this entails are key to the output quality.

3.2 Software Process Improvement Models

The combination of the explained actions of SPI are models e.g. Capability Maturity Models. An advantage to using Capability Maturity Models is that they systematically impose successful practices on different models. Examples of capability maturity models include CMM(I) or SPICE (Hörmann, 2006, p. 5).
Application of the models and actions under the models promote process improvements and thus aid the failure prevention/minimisation effort. In order to be able to effect process improvements, first an inventory check is needed of the actual status. The inventory check takes the form of an assessment. Under the assessment, formal and actually practiced processes are examined separately and correlated with ideal values and criteria under the respective capability maturity model. The correlation output is an action matrix that indicates the problem

areas and processes found. In this way, process improvements may be initiated and implemented in an ideal manner. Fig. 2 shows the interdependencies between processes, process assessments, capability determination (assessment of capability maturity level) and process improvements on applying a capability maturity model such as SPICE or CMM(I).

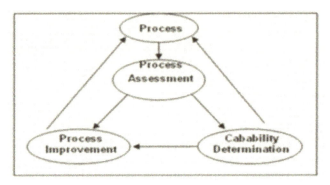

FIG. 2: Software Process Assessment with SPICE according to ISO 15504
(source: Petrasch 1998, p. 119)

Additionally as output, the capability maturity level is determined. Most models differentiate between levels on a range from 1 to 5, 1 to 6 or 1 to 7.
The higher the level within a model, the better the processes concerned are formally defined and practiced.

SPI are important for reducing failure and increasing quality. Late failure detection adds massively to costs. According to various analyses, failure elimination costs, as a variable, multiply by a factor of about five to ten for each phase in the sequence. This means that a failure generated in the initial specification phase that has been identified only as late as in the programming phase becomes n-times more expensive to eliminate by then. The cost growth factor between the initial specification phase and acceptance testing may reach as much as 100 (Balzert 1998, p. 288). The author's own practical experience and analyses confirm this figure. Consequently, SPI should be pursued as the primary aim.

The goal may be complied with much easier by practicing quality control in each phase of the process rather than at the very end of the development chain only (Balzert 1998, p. 287 ff.). Quality has to be generated within the process as opposed to "imposing it" on the product post process. A about 50% of failure occur in the initial design and specification phases (Balzert 1998, p. 289), it is particularly important to concentrate on SPI specifically in the initial phases.

3.3 SPI Manifesto

The new approach for SPI in this paper will support the existing SPI activities including the following 10 statements from the SPI Manifesto in 2010 (SPI-Manifesto 2010). See Table 1.

People	Business	Change
Know the culture and focus on needs	Support the organisation's vision and objectives	Manage the organisational change in your improvement effort
Motivate all people involved	Use dynamic and adaptable models as needed	Ensure all parties understand and agree on process
Base improvement on experience and measurements	Apply risk management	Do not lose focus
Create a learning organisation		

Tab. 1: SPI-Manifesto 2010; (source: SPI-Manifesto 2010)

4 New approach of Software Process Improvements

As SPI involves a lot of different areas/elements e.g. people, culture, organisation, methods, communication etc. it will be considered in this paper as complex network system.

Complexity according to Ulrich und Probst (1988, p. 57) is defined first by the structure, number and variety of and the interrelationships between the different elements in a system and second by variability in time. Grossmann (1992, p. 19) recognises four basic types of systems:

- **Simple systems** (with few components and interrelationships),

- **Intricate systems** (a variety of components and interrelationships, with mostly predetermined system behaviour);

- **Fairly complex systems** (few components and interrelationships which however exhibit a variety in potential behaviour modes and variable cause and effect chains);

- **Highly complex systems** (a variety of components, highly varied interrelationships, a large variety of potential behaviour modes with variable cause and effect chains between the components).

Systemic Perspective on Software Development and SPI

The software development process and SPI are complex network processes with a number of applicable determinants interactions and as such, are to be viewed in its entirety (Frick 1995, p. 1). For examination purposes concerning holistic systemic SPI in and for development process, the determinants or influencing factors need to be identified and analysed.

4.1 Method

The methods for dealing with complexity are subject to 26 criteria according to Grossmann (Grossmann 1992, p. 44). Some of the 26 criteria are (excerpt):
1.   Providing for a large number of components;
2.   Reflecting mutual relationships between the components;
3.   Providing for variability in time;
4.   Providing for changing cause and effect chains;
5.-26. Other criteria.

4.2   Model

There are various models for better dealing with complex systems. The models allow among other things simulations of the different forces and interactions at work in complex systems in order to identify approaches that best facilitate problem solutions (Grossmann 1992, p. 55). Models are a reflection of reality.
In order to be able to effectively deal with complexity and hence facilitate comprehensive holistic SPI, a model has to include both the factual and behaviour-related dimensions. In comprehensive systemic examination, human-related and factual dimensions have to be explored as the determinants and interactions at work falling under both dimensions. Grossmann (1992, p. 59 ff.) examined nine methods/models for dealing with complexity and placed each within a square with factual and behaviour-related dimensions. The method/models for dealing with complex tasks have been conceived by e.g. the following authors:

1. System Dynamics (by Forrester);
2. Thinking in networks (Ulrich, Probst);
3. Sensitivity Model (by Vester).

A conclusion based on assessment/analysis of three of the total of nine concepts (Grossmann 1992, p. 188) is that "Thinking in networks" was selected. It appears to be based on current knowledge and by earning the best assessment grades as viable methods for the task of comprehensive SPI in/for the software development process. Thinking in network relies, according to Ulrich and Probst (1991, p. 25ff.), on seven basic principles. From the seven basic principles, Ulrich and Probst (1991, p. 114ff.) derived the following six steps within the problem solving process.

(1) Defining objectives and modelling the problem situation
(2) Analysing causal chains
(3) Exploring and interpreting possible trends in the future based on current status
(4) Exploring control options
(5) Planning strategies and actions
(6) Implementing the problem solution.

5 Tools for interlinked SPI

Various simulation and practical implementation (operationalization) tools have been derived from the thinking in network method. The tools include:

GAMMA tool and CONSIDEO MODELER.

The GAMMA tool has a long tradition with the Vester (2001) approach. The Consideo Modeler is a new approach but also based on Vester (2007). In this paper / approach the GAMMA tool is used. In the above mention PhD the Consideo Modeler was used. It is very easy to port the approach in this paper to another tool because the basics are for all tools the same.

GAMMA tool

The GAMMA tool is a combined concept and tool for dealing / solving complex problems (Hub 2002, p. 29). The concept refers to the thinking in networks method. The above mentioned six steps within the problem solving process and/or the six steps under the thinking in networks method translate in the GAMMA concept into the following phases:
- Problem identification;
- System modelling;
- System analysis;
- Definition of actions to take.

6 Influence Elements of SPI

The new approach of the SPI is based on selection of 12 (of over 100) important influence elements (Number 2 to 13 in Fig. 3). Number 1 is our goal (SPI). The selection on the above mention elements was done via literature research, empirical researching, own experience and simulation with various numbers of factors. This number of influence elements is enough to explain and use the new approach of SPI in practice. The approach can be expanded later on with much more elements like in the PhD paper.

In Fig. 3, the selected influence elements are presented with the GAMMA tool.

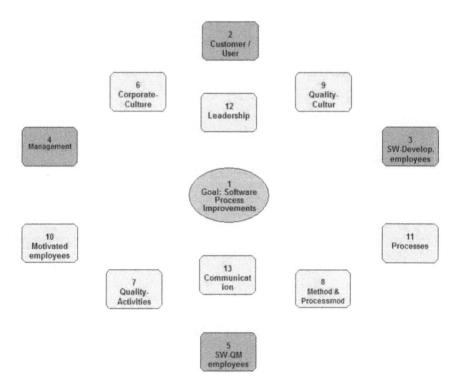

FIG. 3: Elements of Software Process Improvement

The best results for selection of the elements and the interlinking of them will be reached by Group discussions.

6.1 Description of the Elements

(1) *Target Variable*

The target variable is identifiable with the element "**Software Process Improvement**" **(SPI)** in the centre of Fig. 3

- *Elements*

  The following elements are extracts of the elements affect the target variable directly or indirectly.

(2) *Customer/User*

The customer/User is playing an important role in the SPI because they have to define the requirements of the Software (SW). The requirements have to be written in an understandable way and structure for the SW-Development employees/organization. Especially in the definition phase of the SW it is important to integrate the customer in the SW-Development employees/organization for a better transformation process of the requirements.

(3) *SW-Development Employees*

The SW-Development Employees/organization is one of the central persons in the SPI. He has via processes, process-models and methods, the main tasks of the SW-Development. His qualifications have to be very high. On-going training in the SPI is mandatory for better SW and the motivation of the employees.

(4) *Management*

The management of the organization has the task to organise all the processes to reach the goal of the company. Management in the organisation has two main tasks:

Task No. 1 is to leading the employees, motivate them (see motivated people (10)) and to coordinate all tasks that the employees/subordinates can fulfil.

Task Nr. 2 is the "Process of the management". This means planning, organising, staffing and controlling an organisation. Organisation means a group of people or entities.

(5) *SW-QM-employees*

SPI needs highly qualified persons for the quality management tasks. Product quality starts with the requirements analysis and has to support all the SW-Development phases with quality tasks. The SW-QM employees should be integrated in the development process. Job rotation is a very good integration process.

(6)   *Corporate culture*

Corporate Culture is the entirety of shared values, standards, stances and attitudes that shape the decisions, actions and behaviour of the members of the organisation (Gabler, a). Consequently, the attitudes towards successful failure essentially grow out of corporate culture. For further discourse, refer to Schein (2003).

(7)   *Quality-Activities*

For SPI quality activities are necessary e.g. Reviews and FMEA. The application of constructive actions is the base for defect preventions. The lessons learned from the process will improve the SW-processes from project to project and contribute to the SPI.

(8)   *Methods and Process-model*

SW-Development is based on using a method and process-model. There are various methods available but the methods have to be tailored to the SW task. To use CMMI or SPICE will be a very good base for SPI. The author has positive experience by using maturity models.

(9)   *Quality culture*

For successful Software process improvement, the quality culture practiced by the firm is a key, as the quality culture that grows out of corporate culture is an integral part of enterprise quality (Seghezzi 1996, p. 181). Managerial functions should be a role model in quality matters in their everyday stances and attitudes. Quality culture means e.g. customer focus; open for discussing about failures which happen; willing to learn; quality focus as quality is a everyone job (Mc Donald 2008).

(10)   *Motivated employees*

Motivation is interpreted as the cause for a specific human behaviour (Strunz 2001, p. 49). As a result, the employee becomes directed towards a specific objective. Applied to the effort herein, the objective is "to avoid software failures". Available sources e.g. (MC Donald 2008) deal comprehensively with the topic herein.

(11)   *Processes*

The processes hold together all the following critical dimensions (Chrissis 2003): People, procedures, methods, tools and equipment. It is very important that processes have on-going to be improved to do get better Software. A focus on process improvement is necessary to manage the changing world and to be more competitive (Chrissis 2003).

(12) *Leadership*
Leadership is defined in expert sources in a number of different ways, some of which are: Being a role model (Seghezzi 2007, p. 79) and actively dealing with topics (in reference to Strunz 2001, p. 168); Directing staff towards a vision so that they respond in a motivated manner; Making staff understand the context by means of suitable communication (employee orientation).

(13) *Communication*
Within the comprehensive variety of communication, open communication that includes feedback promotes fairness, the will to listen and the readiness to report failures including software failures without fear. Open communication also promotes motivation. Communication should avoid isolated knowledge and should promote upward communication also (Mc Donald 2008).

The next step in network thinking is the interlinking of the elements.

6.2 Interlinked causal interdependencies

The interlinking of the elements is a very important step to see the various influences of each element in the final network.

After the definition of the elements the elements will be interlinked. The interlinked causal interdependencies are shown in Fig. 4. In the following part some causal interdependencies will be explained e.g. the loop with the starting Nr. $4 \rightarrow 10 \rightarrow 3 \rightarrow 8 \rightarrow 1 \rightarrow 10 \rightarrow 6 \rightarrow 4$.
Time delays in the network in figure 4 have a green colour.

(4) *Management $\rightarrow$ (10) Motivated employees*
One of the important management tasks is to motivate the employees. Motivate people is one of the basic elements for SPI.

(10) *Motivated employees $\rightarrow$ (3) SW-Development Organization.*
Motivated employees will drive the whole SW-Development Organization for SPI.

(3) *SW-Development Organization $\rightarrow$ (8) Method& Process-model*
The SW-Development Organization has to use a Method & Process-model to have success in SPI.

(8) *Method & Process-model $\rightarrow$ (1) SPI*
The use of a Method & Process-model has positive influence on the SPI.

(1) *SPI* → *(10) Motivated employees*
The success in SPI will additionally with a time delay, motivate the employees.

(10) *Motivated employees* → *(6) Corporate Culture*
In a long time horizon, motivated employees will slightly increase the corporate culture.

(6) *Corporate Culture* → *(4) Management*
The corporate culture will increase the management attitude to SPI.

(2) Customer/User → (4) Management
The customer has the "obligation" to write down understandable requirements for the supplier.

(12) Leadership → (3) SW-Development & (5) SW-QM employees
Leadership has a strong influence to the employees. Soft skills are the basics for motivation of employees.

(3) SW-Development & SW-QW employees → processes
Employees have created the processes and have to follow them for successful SPI.

6.3 Network of elements and Cross-Impact Matrix

Fig. 4 shows the interlinked elements, effect directions and effect intensities of each element. The interdependencies (arrows), effect intensities (thickness) and a plus or minus sign are indicated. A plus sign before the numerical intensity signifies in addition to the effect direction it promotive effect, a minus sign its inhibitive effect outlined with the GAMMA Software-Tool (Hub 2002).

The blue colour of the interlinked line is a not delayed interaction and the green colour is a delayed interaction.

The network shows that e.g. element No. 7 "Quality Activities" will have a positive influence to No. 1 "Software Process Improvements". Element No. 12 "Leadership" will have a positive influence to No. 5 "Quality Culture". This means that e.g. element No. 1 (SPI) will have a feedback / delayed influence of the positive motivation of the employees.

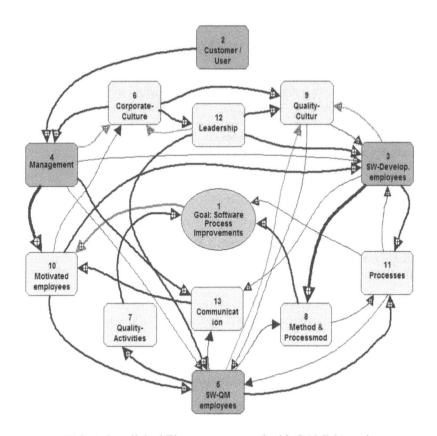

FIG. 4: Interlinked Elements presented with GAMMA tool
(source: the author)

In Fig. 5 the Cross-Impact-Matrix is shown for the identified network factors. The matrix was developed by Vester (2007) and also called "Vester-Papiercomputer". The matrix is used to reflect on all FROM / TO effects / relationships of the elements. The strength of the effect is defined by amount registered.

It can take a value between 1 and 3 (even larger values for some effect relationships). The number 1 represents a weak relationship and 3 represents a strong relationship.

An example effect is the vertical No. 4 (Management) on the horizontal No. 10 (Motivated employee) with the effect strength of 3.

Wirkung VON /AUF	1	2	3	4	5	6	7	8	9	10	11	12	13	Su.E
1. Goal: Software Process Improvements										2				2
2. Customer / User				2										2
3. SW-Develop. employees								3	1		2		1	7
4. Management			1		1	1				3			2	8
5. SW-QM employees							2		1	2			1	6
6. Corporate-Culture				2					2			2		6
7. Quality-Activities	2													2
8. Method Processmodel	2										1			3
9. Quality-Cultur			1		1									2
10. Motivated employees			2		2									4
11. Processes	1		1		1									3
12. Leadership			2		2	1			2					7
13. Communication											2			2
Summe Beeinflussung	5	0	7	4	7	2	2	3	6	7	5	2	4	

FIG. 5 Cross-Impact-Matrix (Vester - Papiercomputer) of the Network

7 Results

The "Influence Matrix" in Fig. 6 shows the position / relevance of every individual influence element in the SPI process. There by, the role of every individual element in the system is clearly identified (Vester 2007, S. 194). Through this representation, the individual interlinking in the system can be determined and the very important elements are visible.

The Matrix has four quadrants with the following impact:

Quadrant active (down right = red) means, that elements in this area influence other elements strongly, but they are not strongly influenced from others;

Quadrant critical (top right = yellow) means, that elements influence other elements strongly and are strongly influenced from others;

Quadrant passive (top left = blue): elements-influencing others only a little, but they are influenced from other elements strongly;

Quadrant buffer (down left = green): elements-influencing others only a little and they are influencing others also only a little.

The calculation of the position of the elements in the matrix is based on the active/passive (active= influencing, passive = influenced) amount of each element. Active amount is the calculation of the values in the line (active sum). Passive amount is the calculation of the values in the column (passive sum).
The highest value is then 100% (see Fig. 5) e.g. the highest value of the active sum of elements is line Nr. 4 (management) with the value 8= 100%. This means that Nr. 4 is placed on the most right position in the matrix. The complete calculation of each elements place in the matrix is explained in Hub (2002). There are two opportunities to analyse the system as the influence matrix can calculated in two ways: 1. Direct influenced elements; 2. cumulated influenced elements.

In Fig. 6 the influencing (Einflussnahme) and influenced (Beeinflussung) elements are shown in the Result Matrix.

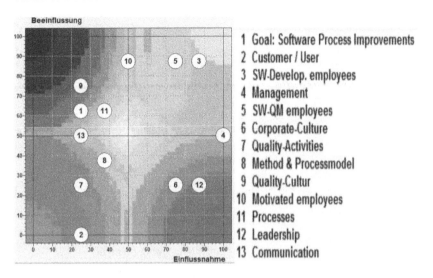

1 Goal: Software Process Improvements
2 Customer / User
3 SW-Develop. employees
4 Management
5 SW-QM employees
6 Corporate-Culture
7 Quality-Activities
8 Method & Processmodel
9 Quality-Cultur
10 Motivated employees
11 Processes
12 Leadership
13 Communication

FIG. 6: Results of the interlinked elements in the influence- matrix

In this paper the direct influenced elements are calculated in the influence-matrix.

We can see that 7 elements are on the left side of the field (Nr. 2, 7, 8, 13, 1, 11 and 9). This means that they are not very strongly influencing the system.

On the right site there are 6 stronger elements (Nr. 6, 12, 4, 3, 5 and 10).

Element No. 6 (Corporate culture) and 12 (Leadership) are very active elements for the target element No. 1 (**Successful Process Improvements=SPI).**

Element No. 1 (SPI) should be more influenced, as it is our goal to improve this

Element No. 4 (Management) has a strong influence in the system, but it is also influenced from other elements (by 50%).

Elements No. 3, No. 5 (and No. 10) are critical elements. This indicates that they can influence the system strongly but reinforcing loops in the system can have a negative influence.

Elements No. 1, 9 11 and 13 are passive elements in the system (less influence). (Element No. 9 is strongly influenced from other elements and has low influence to the system).

Elements No. 2, 7, 8 are balancing the system as the influencing power is low and they are weakly influenced from others.

Further analyses of the interlinking possibilities in the networked system are:

1. Analyse causal chains
2. Feedback analysis
3. Time analysis
4. and others.

to 1. Analyse causal chains:

- How to widen the effects with the interlinking in the network?
- What kind of causal chains will achieve a determined influence level for an effect?
- What are the indirect effect relationships?

There are two possibilities for the functional chain analysis .

a) Which connection is going e.g. to the element No. 1(SPI) to influence it?
b) Which connection is starting from e.g. the element No. 3
    (SW-Development employees) to influence other elements.

In this example we decided to use No. a) Which connection is going to element No. 1 (SPI).
The functional chain analysis shows us in Fig. 7   that 3 elements directly influence the goal SPI. This is No. 7, 8 and 11.

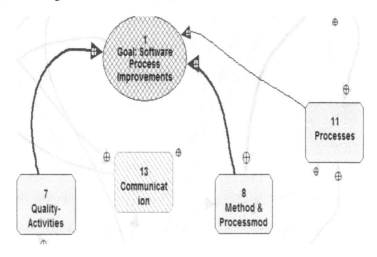

FIG. 7: Analysing of functional chain

To go deeper to analyse the system for various measures it is possible to select e.g. which elements are influencing element No. 8 (Method & Process model).

to 2. Feedback Analysis

This analysis is carried to determine whether there are causal chains that have:

- Desired stabilisation
- Undesired strengthening
- Escalating effects arise.

Feedback analysis is not shown here.

to 3. Time Analysis

Time analysis will not be gone into here.
On the basis of these analyses, strategies / interlinking are derived in the network. This is to clarify which elements are and are not influenced. For which elements do interlinks have a special effect? The optimisation of the system can be made on the basis of different approaches, e.g. which elements influence the active ones in order to strengthen these (optimisation of the entire chain).

Definition of action to take / System intervention

After all of the various analysis, the decision is for the following system / network intervention: Enforce the following activities /connections to test how the system will react.

(10) Motivated employees → (5) SW-QM employees
(5) SW-QM employees → (7) Quality activities
(7) Quality activities → (1) SPI
(10) Motivated employees → (3) SW-Development employees
(3) SW-Development employees → (8) Methods and Process-model
(8) Methods and Process-model → (1) SPI
(9) Quality Culture → (5) SW-QM employees
(9) Quality Culture → (3) SW-Development employees.

In figure 8 the test results are visible. The number of passive and buffer elements decrease from 8 to 5.
The number of active and critical elements increased from 5 to 8.

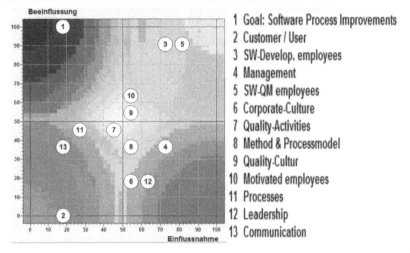

1 Goal: Software Process Improvements
2 Customer / User
3 SW-Develop. employees
4 Management
5 SW-QM employees
6 Corporate-Culture
7 Quality-Activities
8 Method & Processmodel
9 Quality-Cultur
10 Motivated employees
11 Processes
12 Leadership
13 Communication

FIG. 8: Results of the interlinked elements in the matrix influencing and influenced after System modification

The results show that the measures activate more elements. On the left side there are now 5 not so strong elements compared with 7 in Fig. 6. On the right side there are 8 elements. There are 3 more as in Fig. 6.
Nr. 1 (Software Process Improvements) is now a very strong influenced element. The most elements in Fig. 8 "play" after the system intervention a more active role.

8 Conclusion

The results in both influence matrix (in figures 6 and 8) provide indications that the human being represented by management, leadership, employees and culture, are key elements for SPI.

The most significant elements with strong positive effect in successful SPI are No. 4 (Management), No. 6 (Corporate culture) and 12 (Leadership). The No. 3 (Software Develop. employee) and 5 (SW-QM employee) are active but critical elements and need further consideration. The elements No.7 (Quality activities), No. 8 (Methods & Process-model), No. 11 (Processes) and No. 13 (Communication) could be enforced. The customer (2) has a low influence of SPI and is not influenced by any element. The SPI (1) is and has to be a passive element in the system as SPI is our goal and has to be influenced strongly by the elements.

One additional goal of this paper is to visualise different relationships of the elements in the SPI and to contribute to the system thinking in the SPI. The results of the network and influence matrix should not be interpreted very precisely, but it is an important indication of the interlinking of the elements and its priority for SPI.

The reader has to be aware that the source of the shown results are depending of the interlinked Elements (Fig.4). The best approach of interlinking the elements in practice is doing it in a small group of Software- and Quality experts.

This new approach will not replace the existing SPI methods but support it from a holistic view. The holistic / networked investigation gives us an indication which elements / action in the SPI process are strong / important or not strong / important.

Generally, a note is due that any actions and approach expansions made need to be verified for their interlinking effects and balanced accordingly as the elements function in a matrix of mutual relationships and consequently also need assessment in a relationship matrix.

It is worthwhile for further research on this system e.g. deeper analysis or the system expansion with additional elements.

References

Balzert, H.F. (1998). Lehrbuch der Software-Technik; Software-Management, Software-Qualitätssicherung, Unternehmensmodellierung. Spektrum, Akademischer Verlag Heidelberg/Berlin

Chrissis (2003). CMMI Guidelines for Process Integration and Product Improvement, Tenth printing, March 2006, Pearson Education, Inc. Boston, MA. USA

CONSIDEO Modeler (2009). Modellierungssoftware von Consideo GmbH, D-23562 Lübeck

Grossmann, C. (1992). Komplexitätsbewältigung im Management; Anleitungen, integrierte Methodik und Anwendungsbeispiele; Verlag GCN, Winterthur

Forrester, J.W.: World Dynamics, Wright-Allen-Press Cambridge; USA, MA 1971

Frick, A. (1995). Der Softwareentwicklungs-Prozess; ganzheitliche Sicht; Grundlagen zu Entwicklungs-Prozess-Modellen, Hanser Verlag München 1995

Gabler_a. Gabler online Wirtschaftslexikon

Hörmann, K./Dittmann, L./Hindel, B. (2006). SPICE in der Praxis; Interpretationshilfe für Anwender und Assessoren, basierend auf ISO/IEC 15504, dpunkt.Verlag, Heidelberg

Hindel, B. (2009) Vorlesung „Praktische Softwaretechnik" Friedrich-Alexander-Universität Erlangen-Nürnberg

Hub, H. (2002) GAMMA Software, Praxisbeispiele zum ganzheitlich vernetzten Denken; DMG Verlag, Nürtingen 2002

Masing, W. (2007). Handbuch Qualitätsmanagement; Herausgegeben von T. Pfeifer/R. Schmitt, Hanser Verlag München

Mc. Donald, M./Musson, R./Smith, R. 2008. The Practical Guide to Defect Prevention. Techniques to Meet the Demand for More Reliable Software; Microsoft Press; Redmond, Wa, USA 2008

Petrasch, R. (1998). Einführung in das Software-Qualitätsmanagement; Software-Qualität, Softwaremanagement, Normen und Standards, Logos-Verlag Berlin 1998

Schein, E.H. (2003). Organisationskultur; The Ed Schein Corporate Culture Survival Guide; MIT/Cambridge USA; Edition HumanistischePsychologie, BergischGladbach

Seghezzi, H. D. (1996). Integriertes Qualitätsmanagement; Das St. Galler Konzept München; Hanser Verlag München

Seghezzi, H.D. (2007). Integriertes Qualitätsmanagement; Der St. Galler Ansatz; Hanser Verlag München

SPI- Manifesto (2010). Software Process Improvement, eurospi.net 10.12.2010

Strunz, H. / Dorsch, M. (2001). Management; Managementwissen für Studium und Praxis, Oldenburg Wissenschaftsverlag München

Ulrich & Probst 1988 & 1991. Anleitung zum ganzheitlichen Denken und Handeln; Ein Brevier für Führungskräfte, Verlag Paul Haupt, Bern/Stuttgart 1988 und 1991

Unmüßig, A. (2012). Ganzheitlich vernetzte Fehlerprävention im Software-Entwicklungsprozess, Verlag SHAKER, D-Aachen 2012, ISBN: 978-3-8440-1188-3

Vester, F. (2007). Die Kunst vernetzt zu denken; Ideen und Werkzeuge für einen neuen Umgang mit Komplexität, dtv Verlag, München

Vester, F. (2001). Die Kunst vernetzt zu denken; Ideen und Werkzeuge für einen neuen Umgang mit Komplexität, dtv Verlag, München

Wallmüller, E. (2001). Software Qualitätsmanagement in der Praxis, Hanser Verlag München